COOKING TOGETHER:
RECIPES FOR PARENTS AND KIDS

120 TASTY RECIPES

BARBOUR

© 2010 by Barbour Publishing, Inc.

Compiled by MariLee Parrish.

ISBN 978-1-60260-898-6

Published by Barbour Publishing, Inc., P.O. Box 719, Uhrichsville, Ohio 44683, www.barbourbooks.com

Our mission is to publish and distribute inspirational products offering exceptional value and biblical encouragement to the masses.

Member of the
Evangelical Christian
Publishers Association

Printed in China.

INSPIRATION
at your fingertips!

Looking for a new way to connect with your kids? This book is for you. Within these pages, you'll find dozens of tasty recipes that are easy to prepare with the help of little hands and are a delight to share with family and friends.

Finding a recipe is as easy as flipping through the book. Along the edge of each page, you'll see a color that corresponds to one of five categories:

No Baking Required . . . . . .(p. 5)	
In the Microwave . . . . . . (p. 33)	
On the Stove . . . . (p. 61)	
In the Oven . . . . (p. 89)	
Snacks, Sweets & Drinks . .(p. 117)	

So set this little book on your countertop, flip page after page for new culinary inspiration and kitchen tips and tricks, and you might just find a little encouragement for your soul in the process. Enjoy!

No Baking Required

You feed them from the abundance of your own house, letting them drink from your river of delights.
PSALM **36:8** NLT

Baking
No Baking

DINNER SALAD

1 head lettuce
½ cup cheddar cheese, shredded
1 small tomato, chopped
½ cup fresh broccoli, chopped

···

Show your child how to break apart the lettuce and wash it in the sink. Then add remaining ingredients and toss. Serve with your favorite dressing.

BLUEBERRY CREAM CHEESE BAGEL

1 whole-wheat bagel
1 tablespoon cream cheese
4 to 5 fresh blueberries

....

Toast the bagel and top with cream cheese. Press the blueberries into the cream cheese and enjoy.

NO BAKING REQUIRED

GRAPE CHICKEN SALAD

2 (5 ounce) cans chicken breast, drained
$\frac{1}{4}$ cup mayonnaise
$\frac{1}{4}$ cup sweet onion, chopped
6 to 8 red seedless grapes, cut in half
$\frac{1}{4}$ cup chopped walnuts
1 teaspoon seasoned salt

. . . .

Mix all ingredients together and serve on lettuce or toast.

JAKE'S FAVORITE BREAKFAST

1 frozen whole-grain waffle
1 tablespoon strawberry cream cheese
½ ripe banana

....

Toast the waffle and spread with cream cheese.
Top with slices of banana and serve.

APPLE PEANUT BUTTER ROLLS

4 slices white bread, crusts removed
½ cup peanut butter
¼ cup apple butter
¼ cup shredded apples

. . . .

Roll each slice of bread with a rolling pin until flat.
Spread two tablespoons peanut butter on each
slice of bread. Top each slice with one tablespoon
apple butter and one tablespoon shredded apples.
Roll up sandwiches and cut into slices.

PEANUT BUTTER & JELLY ROLL-UPS

4 slices whole-wheat bread, crusts removed
½ cup peanut butter
¼ cup grape jelly
1 banana, sliced

....

Roll each slice of bread with a rolling pin until flat.
Spread two tablespoons peanut butter on each
slice of bread. Top each slice with one tablespoon
jelly and slices of banana. Roll up sandwiches and
cut into slices.

4 to 6 slices turkey pepperoni
1 slice provolone cheese
1 flour tortilla

· ·

Place pepperoni and cheese on tortilla and roll up.
Dip in warm pizza sauce.

HANDY CONVERSIONS

1 teaspoon = 5 milliliters
1 tablespoon = 15 milliliters
1 fluid ounce = 30 milliliters
1 cup = 250 milliliters
1 pint = 2 cups (or 16 fluid ounces)
1 quart = 4 cups (or 2 pints or 32 fluid ounces)
1 gallon = 16 cups (or 4 quarts)
1 peck = 8 quarts
1 bushel = 4 pecks
1 pound = 454 grams

Quick Chart

Fahrenheit	Celsius
250°–300°	121°–149°
300°–325°	149°–163°
325°–350°	163°–177°
375°	191°
400°– 425°	204°–218°

TUNA SALAD

1 (5 ounce) can albacore tuna, drained
1 tablespoon relish
2 tablespoons mayonnaise

....

Mix all ingredients together and spread on bread
or crackers.

BACON CHICKEN SALAD

2 (5 ounce) cans chicken breast, drained
¼ cup mayonnaise
¼ cup sweet onion, chopped
3 tablespoons real bacon bits
1 teaspoon seasoned salt

. . . .

Mix all ingredients together and serve with lettuce and tomato on toast.

FRUIT SANDWICH

NO BAKING REQUIRED

½ cup cottage cheese
1 cup cream cheese, softened
¾ cup crushed pineapple, drained
2 slices honey-wheat bread

....

Combine all ingredients and spread on bread.

ANTS ON AN INNER TUBE

1 bagel
2 tablespoons peanut butter
1 tablespoon raisins

Toast bagel and spread each half with 1 tablespoon peanut butter. Top each half with raisins.

CREAM CHEESE TURKEY BAGEL

1 tablespoon cream cheese
1 bagel
1 slice deli turkey

Spread cream cheese on bagel and top with turkey. Add slices of bacon and tomato if desired.

APPLE CHICKEN SALAD

2 (5 ounce) cans chicken breast, drained
¼ cup mayonnaise
¼ cup sweet onion, chopped
1 small apple, chopped
1 teaspoon seasoned salt
4 slices Swiss cheese
Croissants

Mix chicken, mayonnaise, onion, apple, and salt together. Slice the croissants and place 1 slice of cheese on each. Top with desired amount of chicken salad.

ITALIAN HAM SANDWICH

¼ cup bagged salad mix with carrots
1 tablespoon mozzarella cheese
1 tablespoon Italian dressing
2 bread slices, toasted
Deli ham slices

....

Mix ingredients together in a bowl and place on toasted bread. Top with deli ham slices.

PEANUT BUTTER AND HONEY SANDWICH

1 tablespoon honey
2 tablespoons peanut butter
2 bread slices, toasted

....

Combine honey and peanut butter in bowl. Stir well. Spread on toast and top with sliced apples or bananas if desired.

NO BAKING REQUIRED

START SIMPLE

Begin your *Cooking Together* experience by starting with quick and easy tasks in the kitchen: mashing potatoes, making peanut butter and jelly, mixing chocolate milk, and wiping off the counters. Then try some of the more challenging recipes.

Quick Tip

KIDS' HERO SANDWICHES

1 tablespoon mayonnaise
1 tablespoon mustard
4 hot dog buns
4 slices deli turkey
4 slices provolone cheese
4 slices deli ham
2 tomatoes, thinly sliced

....

Spread a thin layer of mayonnaise and mustard
on each hot dog bun. Top with desired amount of
remaining ingredients.

TURKEY PESTO SANDWICHES

2 tablespoons mayonnaise
¼ cup pesto
3 bagels
3 slices cheddar cheese
3 slices lettuce
3 to 6 thin slices deli turkey
1 small tomato, sliced

Mix mayonnaise and pesto. Spread on bagels. Top with remaining ingredients.

CHICKEN COBB SANDWICHES

3 cups cooked chicken, cut into thin strips
2 tomatoes, chopped
2 avocados, peeled and chopped
4 slices bacon, cooked and crumbled
½ cup blue cheese, crumbled
¼ cup ranch salad dressing
2 cups baby spinach leaves
Flour tortillas

....

Combine all ingredients and mix well. Spoon onto flour tortillas and serve.

EASY PASTA SALAD

1 pound prepared rotini pasta
1 ripe avocado, peeled and chopped
4 string cheese sticks, chopped
10 to 12 cherry tomatoes, halved
¼ cup Italian dressing

· ·

Mix all ingredients together and chill.

CUCUMBER SANDWICH

1 ounce cream cheese
½ cup mayonnaise
1 small onion, chopped fine
½ teaspoon salt
1 medium cucumber, seeded and sliced
Bread slices or crackers

....

Mix all ingredients together except cucumber.
Spread on bread or crackers and top with
cucumbers.

DEVILED EGGS

4 hard-boiled eggs
1 tablespoon relish
2 tablespoons mayonnaise
Paprika

....

Crack eggs by gently tapping them on the counter
and peeling off shells. Cut eggs in half and drop
yolks into small bowl. Using a fork, mash yolks
with relish and mayonnaise. Fill egg halves with
yolk mixture and sprinkle with paprika.

EASY POTATO SALAD

½ cup mayonnaise
1 teaspoon cider vinegar
1 tablespoon sugar
1 teaspoon mustard
1 teaspoon salt
¼ teaspoon pepper
6 large potatoes, cooked, peeled, and chopped
1 small onion, chopped
2 stalks celery, chopped

....

Whisk first four ingredients together. Add salt and pepper. Pour over vegetables and toss to coat. Refrigerate.

CUCUMBER AND TOMATO SALAD

1 large cucumber, sliced
2 large tomatoes, chopped
1 small sweet onion, chopped
2 tablespoons zesty Italian dressing
1 tablespoon sugar

Mix all ingredients and chill 30 minutes before serving.

Each new culinary skill you share with your children is another step in their journey to become proficient in the kitchen. Start them on a road of good nutrition at a young age, and you'll see them reap the health benefits throughout life.

Quick Tip

PISTACHIO SALAD

1 (3½ ounce) package pistachio instant pudding
1 cup mini marshmallows
1 (16 ounce) can crushed pineapple with juice
1 (8 ounce) container whipped cream

....

Stir pudding and marshmallows into pineapple and juice. Mix in whipped cream. Pour into bowl or mold and chill.

In the Microwave

Delight yourself in the LORD and he will give you the desires of your heart.
PSALM 37:4 NIV

REBECCA'S TOASTED CHEESE SANDWICH

2 slices bread
1 slice American cheese

....

Toast bread to desired darkness and place a slice of cheese between them. Microwave it for 15 seconds—the cheese is melted and warm, and your toast is still crunchy!

EGG IN A TOMATO

1 large tomato
½ teaspoon butter
Dash salt
1 egg
1 teaspoon cheddar cheese, shredded

. . . .

Slice off the tomato stem and scoop out seeds
and pulp. Place tomato in microwavable bowl.
Place butter and salt inside the tomato and add
the egg. Pierce the yolk with a toothpick. Add
cheese. Place the top slice back on the tomato.
Microwave on medium-high 1 minute 45 seconds,
or until egg is almost cooked. Let stand 1 minute.

BACON, CHEESE, & TOMATO SANDWICH

3 slices bacon
3 slices whole wheat toast
2 tablespoons mayonnaise
1 large tomato, sliced
3 slices cheddar cheese

Microwave bacon according to package directions. Place toast on plate and spread with mayonnaise. Top with tomato and cheese slices. Crumble bacon and sprinkle over top. Microwave on high for 1 minute or until cheese begins to melt.

MEAT LOAF WEDGES

1½ pounds ground beef
1 egg yolk, slightly beaten
⅓ cup milk
½ cup oats
1½ teaspoons salt
¼ teaspoon pepper

Mix beef, egg yolk, milk, oats, and seasonings.
Combine lightly but thoroughly. Shape meat
mixture and place in microwavable baking dish.
Cut meat mixture into wedges and push each
wedge apart slightly. Cook on high 12 minutes,
rotating halfway through. Let stand 2 minutes and
serve with ketchup.

ASIAN MEAT LOAF

1½ pounds lean ground beef
1 large egg
1 cup soft bread crumbs
2 teaspoons parsley
1 tablespoon onion, chopped
2 tablespoons brown sugar, divided
2 tablespoons soy sauce, divided
¼ teaspoon ginger
1 tablespoon honey

Combine beef, egg, crumbs, parsley, onion, 1 tablespoon brown sugar, 1 tablespoon soy sauce, and ginger. Mix well. Press into a microwavable loaf pan. Microwave on high 12 minutes. Rotate once. Invert onto a plate. Mix remaining ingredients and spread on top. Microwave on high 2 additional minutes.

CORN CHIP CASSEROLE

½ cup corn chips
1 (7 ounce) can chili with beans
½ cup cheddar Jack cheese, shredded

••

Place corn chips in microwavable bowl. Top with chili. Heat on high for 2 minutes. Stir well. Sprinkle cheese on top. Heat on medium power 45 seconds or until cheese is melted. Sprinkle with chopped onion if desired.

MINI PIZZAS

2 cups pizza sauce
1 (6 count) package English muffins
Sliced pepperoni
2 cups mozzarella cheese, shredded

Spoon sauce onto open-face muffins. Place desired amount of sliced pepperoni on each muffin. Top with desired amount of cheese. Microwave on high 2 minutes or until cheese is melted.

WASH UP!

Have your children create and decorate
a sign as a reminder to always wash your
hands before handling food. Post one near
your kitchen sink and in the bathroom.

························ (Quick Tip) ························

BACON & SWISS SANDWICHES

5 slices bacon
4 slices whole-wheat toast
⅓ cup mayonnaise
Dash dill weed
4 slices Swiss cheese

Microwave bacon according to package directions. Place toast on a plate and spread with mayonnaise; sprinkle with dill. Top with bacon and cheese slices. Microwave on high for 1 minute or until cheese begins to melt. Top with sliced tomato and lettuce, if desired.

HOMEMADE POTATO CHIPS

3 medium red potatoes,
   washed and sliced extra thin
$\frac{1}{4}$ cup olive oil
1 teaspoon salt
Dash garlic powder

....

Layer three paper towels on microwavable
plate. Brush potato slices on both sides with
olive oil and lightly sprinkle with salt and garlic
powder. Arrange on prepared plate; do not
overlap. Microwave on high for 3 minutes. Turn
each chip over with fork. Microwave for 2 to 3
minutes longer or until chips are dry and crunchy.
Cool and serve.

CORN ON THE COB

IN THE MICROWAVE

1 ear corn, husked and cleaned

....

Wrap the ear of corn in a moist paper towel and place on a microwave safe dinner plate. Cook in microwave for 5 minutes on high. Carefully remove paper towel. Spread with butter and add a dash of salt if desired.

BRUSCHETTA DIP

2 tomatoes, chopped
1 small sweet onion, chopped
1 teaspoon garlic salt
¼ teaspoon basil
1 teaspoon fresh parsley, chopped
¼ cup olive oil
1 (8 ounce) wheel Brie cheese

....

Mix tomatoes, onion, garlic, basil, parsley, and olive oil. Cover and chill in the refrigerator at least 1 hour. Remove top layer of rind from Brie. Place in microwavable bowl and microwave on high 1 minute, or until the cheese begins to soften. Spoon tomato mixture over the cheese. Microwave on high 1 additional minute. Serve immediately with toast or crackers.

PIZZA DIP

8 ounces cream cheese, softened
½ teaspoon oregano
1 cup mozzarella cheese, shredded
1 cup spaghetti sauce
2 tablespoons green bell pepper, chopped
1 cup pepperoni
2 tablespoons black olives, sliced

....

Mix together cream cheese and oregano. Spread
mixture into a shallow microwavable dish. Sprinkle
½ cup mozzarella cheese on top of cream
cheese mixture. Spread the spaghetti sauce over
all. Sprinkle with remaining cheese. Top with
green pepper, pepperoni, and olives. Cover and
microwave 5 minutes. Serve hot with breadsticks.

MELTED BEEF WRAP

1 teaspoon mayonnaise
1 tortilla
3 to 4 slices deli roast beef
1 slice cheddar cheese
¼ cup baby spinach leaves
2 tablespoons tomatoes, chopped

· ·

Spread mayonnaise onto tortilla. Top with remaining ingredients and roll up. Microwave on high 1 minute or until cheese is melted.

SPANISH RICE

6 slices bacon cooked and crumbled,
   reserve drippings
1 cup minute rice, uncooked
1 (16 ounce) can tomatoes, undrained
1 medium onion, chopped
1 cup tomato juice
1/4 cup green bell pepper, chopped
1 tablespoon fresh parsley, chopped
1/4 teaspoon pepper
1/4 teaspoon salt

. . . .

Pour bacon drippings into microwavable bowl;
add onion and rice. Microwave on high 3 to 4
minutes or until lightly browned. Stir in remaining
ingredients and cooked bacon. Cover and
microwave on high 8 minutes or until rice is
tender.

EASY CHEESY TOAST

1 slice bread, toasted
¼ cup cheese, shredded
Dash garlic salt

··

Cover toast with cheese and dash of garlic salt.
Microwave 20 seconds or until cheese is melted.

KITCHEN TIME =
TEACHING TIME

To prepare for each new recipe, read through the ingredients and directions with your kids and explain any new words or kitchen techniques you'll be doing. Soon you'll have a miniature chef in your kitchen!

Quick
Tip

CRUNCHY BANANA WRAP

1 flour tortilla
2 tablespoons crunchy peanut butter
1 small banana, sliced

....

Spread peanut butter on the tortilla and top with banana slices. Fold tortilla in half and microwave 25 seconds.

STUFFED SWEET POTATOES

4 sweet potatoes, washed and pricked with fork
1 (15 ounce) can black beans, rinsed
1 (16 ounce) can tomatoes and sweet onions
¼ cup reduced-fat sour cream
¼ cup fresh cilantro, chopped

Microwave potatoes on high for 15 minutes or until tender. Combine beans and canned tomatoes. Microwave on high 2 to 3 minutes. Cut a small slit in each potato and press to make a well in the center. Spoon bean mixture into the well. Top each with a dollop of sour cream and a sprinkle of cilantro.

CHILI CHEESE DIP

8 ounces cream cheese, softened
1 (15 ounce) can chili
1 cup cheddar cheese, shredded

∙∙

Spread cream cheese in microwaveable dish. Top
with an even layer of chili and sprinkle cheddar
cheese over all. Microwave on high 5 minutes, or
until the cheese has melted. Serve with corn chips.

MORNING SCRAMBLE

1 large potato, peeled and diced
¼ cup onion, chopped
¼ cup green bell pepper, chopped
4 eggs
¼ cup milk
⅛ teaspoon salt
⅛ teaspoon pepper
⅛ teaspoon garlic salt

Combine potato, onion, and green pepper in 9-inch microwavable pie plate. Cover and microwave on high for 5 minutes, or until potato is tender. In separate bowl, beat eggs, milk, salt, pepper, and garlic salt. Pour over potatoes in pie plate. Cover and microwave on high 4 minutes, stirring after 2 minutes. Let stand covered 1 minute.

CHICKEN LASAGNA

¼ cup cilantro, chopped
½ cup onion, chopped
2 cups shredded cheddar cheese, divided
1 (28 ounce) can enchilada sauce
12 tortillas
8 ounces cream cheese, softened
3 cups cooked chicken, shredded

Mix cilantro, onion, and 1 cup cheddar cheese. Spread ⅔ cup enchilada sauce in microwavable dish. Pour remaining sauce into large bowl. Dip 4 tortillas into sauce and arrange in baking pan. Spread ⅓ of the cream cheese over tortillas. Top with 1 cup chicken. Repeat layers twice. Top with remaining sauce and cheddar cheese. Cover and microwave on high for 13 minutes or until heated through.

BROCCOLI BAKE

1 (10 ounce) can cream of broccoli soup
½ cup milk
½ teaspoon soy sauce
Dash salt
Dash pepper
1 (20 ounce) package frozen broccoli cuts, thawed
1 (3 ounce) can french-fried onions

Combine soup, milk, soy sauce, salt, and pepper.
Stir in broccoli and ½ can of onions. Cover.
Microwave on high 10 minutes, stirring and
rotating halfway through. Top with remaining
onions. Microwave uncovered 1 additional minute.

GREEN BEAN CASSEROLE

3 (10 ounce) cans french-style green beans,
  drained
1 (10 ounce) can cream of mushroom soup
¼ teaspoon salt
⅛ teaspoon pepper
2 cups shredded cheddar cheese
1 cup french-fried onions

....

Place green beans into greased microwavable
dish. Add mushroom soup, salt, and pepper. Add
cheese. Top with french-fried onions. Heat in
microwave 10 minutes on medium-high or until
cheese is melted and mixture is warm.

EASY MORNING MUFFINS

½ cup milk
½ cup vegetable oil
2 eggs
½ cup sugar
2 cups flour
1 tablespoon baking powder
½ teaspoon salt
⅛ teaspoon cinnamon

....

Combine milk, oil, eggs, and sugar. Mix well. Add remaining ingredients and stir just until flour is moistened. Line 6-cup microwavable muffin pan with paper cups. Fill ⅔ full. Cook on medium for 4 minutes. Let stand 5 minutes. Sprinkle with extra cinnamon and sugar if desired.

Assign each child a special task every time you cook or bake together. Have fruit and vegetables to wash? Crown one child prince (or princess) of produce and address him as "Your Highness." Get creative as you assign tasks like stirring, pouring, measuring, and cleaning up afterward.

OMELET IN A MUG

2 eggs
2 tablespoons milk
Dash salt
Dash pepper
2 tablespoons cheddar cheese, shredded

In small bowl, combine eggs, milk, salt, and pepper. Beat well. Pour into 16-ounce microwavable mug or other dish. Microwave on high 1 minute. Stir and top with cheese. Microwave for an additional 30 seconds or until eggs are firm. Stir and serve.

On the Stove

*Great are the works of the Lord; they are
pondered by all who delight in them.*
Psalm 111:2 NIV

TURKEY QUESADILLAS

4 flour tortillas
4 teaspoons butter
Dijon mustard
8 deli turkey slices
2 cups cheddar Jack cheese, shredded

··

Spread one side of each tortilla with one teaspoon
butter. Spread mustard on other side. Add 2
turkey breast slices and top with ½ cup cheese.
Fold in half. Place quesadillas, buttered side down,
in nonstick skillet. Cook 1 minute on each side or
until golden brown.

GRILLED BACON AND CHEESE

Butter
4 slices wheat bread
8 slices cheddar cheese
4 slices bacon, cooked

....

Spread butter on one side of each slice of bread.
Fill each sandwich with cheese and bacon. Cook
in skillet 2 minutes on first side, then flip and cook
another 2 minutes or until golden brown.

CHEESY BEEF-A-RONI

1 pound ground beef, browned
1 (15 ounce) can sloppy joe sauce
¾ cup elbow macaroni, cooked according to
    package directions
1 cup cheese

In a large skillet, add first three ingredients and simmer 5 minutes or until heated through. Top with cheese.

SAUSAGE OMELET

6 eggs, beaten
Butter
½ teaspoon salt
¼ teaspoon pepper
4 sausage links, cooked and sliced
½ cup cheddar cheese, shredded

....

Scramble eggs in a buttered skillet. Add salt,
pepper, sausage, and cheese. Cook 4 additional
minutes until sausage is heated through and
cheese is melted.

HAM AND CHEESE BREAKFAST SANDWICHES

8 eggs
¼ cup milk
Butter
1 small sweet onion, chopped
6 slices deli ham
Salt and pepper to taste
6 slices American cheese
8 slices white bread, toasted and buttered
1 medium tomato, sliced thin

. . . .

Scramble eggs with milk in a buttered skillet. Add onion, ham, salt, and pepper. Cook for 5 to 6 minutes. Add cheese. Allow eggs to sit until cheese is melted. Scoop onto buttered toast and add tomato; top with toast. Makes 4 sandwiches.

BREAKFAST PIZZA

4 eggs
¼ teaspoon salt
Dash pepper
4 whole wheat English muffins, split
Butter
8 slices cheddar cheese
2 tomatoes, sliced

Lightly beat eggs with salt and pepper. Pour into baking dish. Soak English muffin halves in eggs, cut side down. In a buttered skillet, cook muffin halves, cut side down, on medium heat 2 to 3 minutes or until egg is cooked. Flip and place 1 slice of cheese on each. Top with tomato slices and heat until cheese is melted.

GRILLED CHEESE AND TOMATO SANDWICH

Butter
2 slices bread
1 slice tomato
Cheddar cheese, cut into four thin slices

Butter one side of each bread slice. In a skillet, melt a small pat of butter over low heat. Assemble the sandwich, buttered sides facing out, and use a spatula to place it into the skillet. When the cheese has started to melt, carefully flip it over. When the sandwich is a golden brown on both sides, turn off the heat and remove it from the pan.

PICKY EATERS

If you have a picky eater or two in your family, allowing them to be involved is a great way to get them interested in eating what's for dinner. Start by having them help plan a menu, give them the opportunity to pick out ingredients at the grocery store, and give them ownership in helping to prepare the food. Pretty soon your picky eaters will be clean-platers!

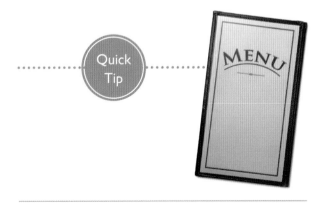

Quick Tip

MENU

SKILLET CHICKEN CASSEROLE

2 tablespoons butter
2 cups chicken, cooked and diced
2 cups rice, cooked
½ bag frozen broccoli, carrot, and cauliflower mix
1 cup cheese, shredded
1 teaspoon salt

Melt butter in large skillet. Stir in chicken, rice, and vegetables. Cook 5 minutes on medium-high heat or until heated through. Stir in cheese and serve. Salt to taste.

PORK SKILLET DINNER

1 tablespoon vegetable oil
¾ pound pork tenderloin, cut into strips
2 (3 ounce) packages pork-flavored ramen
   noodles
1½ cups water
1 medium bell pepper, chopped
1 cup broccoli florets
1 small sweet onion, chopped
1 tablespoon fresh parsley, chopped
1 tablespoon soy sauce

....

Heat oil in skillet over medium-high heat. Add pork and stir-fry about 5 minutes or until pork is no longer pink. Stir broken noodles, seasonings from flavor packets, and remaining ingredients into pork. Heat to boiling. Boil 3 to 4 minutes, stirring occasionally, until noodles are soft.

TEX-MEX
MAC 'N' CHEESE

ON THE STOVE

3 cups pasta
3 cups water
1 cup evaporated milk
1 red bell pepper, chopped
1 small sweet onion, chopped
¼ cup black olives, sliced
1 (4 ounce) can diced green chilies
1 cup Monterey Jack cheese, shredded

Combine pasta and water in large saucepan and bring to a boil. Cook, stirring occasionally, 8 to 10 minutes or until pasta is tender and water is almost gone. Add evaporated milk, red bell pepper, onion, olives, and green chilies. Bring to a boil. Reduce heat to medium. Cook mixture 5 to 7 minutes until sauce has thickened, stirring occasionally. Top with cheese.

BEEF TACO SKILLET

1 pound ground beef, browned
1 (10 ounce) can tomato soup
1 cup chunky salsa
½ cup water
8 flour tortillas, cut into 1-inch pieces
1 cup Monterey Jack cheese, shredded

In large skillet, add beef, soup, salsa, water, tortillas, and half the cheese. Heat to a boil. Cover and cook over low heat 5 minutes or until hot. Top with remaining cheese.

ON THE STOVE

CHICKEN AND POTATO SKILLET DINNER

3 tablespoons oil
4 cups frozen, diced hash browns
1 cup onion, chopped
¾ cup bell pepper, chopped
2 cups cooked chicken, diced
1 cup milk
2 chicken bouillon cubes
2 teaspoons flour
¼ teaspoon pepper
1 cup cheese, shredded

Heat oil in large skillet over medium heat. Cook potatoes, onion, and pepper 12 minutes, until potatoes are cooked. Add chicken. Meanwhile, combine milk, bouillon, flour, and pepper in small saucepan. Cook over medium heat, stirring constantly, 4 minutes or until mixture thickens. Pour sauce over chicken. Top with cheese.

MUSHROOM BEEF SKILLET

1 pound ground beef, browned
1 (10 ounce) can cream of mushroom soup
¼ cup water
1 tablespoon Worcestershire sauce
⅛ teaspoon pepper
1 cup potatoes, cooked and chopped
1 cup frozen carrots, thawed

In large skillet, combine all ingredients and cook on medium-high 8 to 10 minutes or until heated through.

ON THE STOVE

SKILLET GARLIC CHICKEN DINNER

ON THE STOVE

1 (14 ounce) can chicken broth
1 teaspoon garlic salt
¾ cup regular long-grain white rice, uncooked
1 (16 ounce) bag frozen broccoli, cauliflower, and carrots
⅓ cup grated Parmesan cheese
2 cups cooked chicken, diced

. . . .

In large skillet coated with cooking spray, combine broth, garlic salt, rice, and vegetables. Heat to a boil. Cover and cook over low heat 15 minutes. Stir in cheese. Add chicken. Cover and cook 10 minutes or until heated through.

2 tablespoons Italian dressing
¼ cup orange juice
2 tablespoons soy sauce
¼ cup oil
1 pound beef sirloin, cut into strips
1 (16 ounce) package frozen mixed vegetables, thawed

- -

Mix salad dressing, juice, soy sauce, and oil until well blended. Heat large skillet over medium-high heat. Add meat and 1 tablespoon of the dressing mixture; cook 5 minutes or until meat is cooked through. Add vegetables and remaining dressing mixture. Cook and stir until vegetables are tender-crisp. Serve over hot cooked rice.

Introduce your kids to cooking by preparing your favorite meals together. Then, once they learn the basics, start introducing new recipes. Soon you'll have new favorites to add to the list!

Quick Tip

CHICKEN OLÉ

1 tablespoon vegetable oil
1 pound boneless, skinless chicken breasts,
    cut into strips
1 (16 ounce) can corn, drained
2 cups chunky salsa
1 (4 ounce) can chopped green chilies, undrained
1½ teaspoons chili powder
1 teaspoon onion powder

In large skillet, heat oil over medium-high heat. Add chicken strips and cook 5 minutes, stirring frequently. Stir in corn, salsa, chilies, chili powder, and onion powder. Heat to a boil. Reduce heat to medium-low and cook 10 minutes, stirring occasionally. Serve with tortilla chips and cheese.

ON THE STOVE

16 ounces bowtie pasta, prepared
1 pound lean ground beef, browned
1 (24 ounce) jar spaghetti sauce
2 cups mozzarella cheese

Prepare pasta according to package directions.
Brown beef and drain. Add pasta and spaghetti
sauce and heat through. Top with cheese.

SODA POP CHICKEN

1 cup cola
1 cup prepared barbecue sauce
1 ½ pounds boneless, skinless chicken breast pieces

Mix cola and barbecue sauce in large saucepan or Dutch oven. Add chicken. Cover and cook over medium heat 45 minutes or until chicken is tender and no longer pink. Serve with rice.

EASY CHEESE SOUP

1 cup water
1 medium onion, finely chopped
¼ cup celery, finely chopped
½ cup carrots, finely chopped
2 cups chicken broth
1 cup sharp cheddar cheese, shredded
½ cup half-and-half
Salt to taste

....

Bring water to a boil in large saucepan. Add vegetables and reduce the heat to low. Simmer, covered, 15 to 20 minutes or until the vegetables are tender. Add remaining ingredients and mix well. Cook until heated through. Do not boil.

PASTA AND BEAN SOUP

1 onion, chopped
1 tablespoon olive oil
1 teaspoon garlic salt
¼ teaspoon thyme
½ teaspoon oregano
3 beef bouillon cubes
4 cups water
½ cup bowtie pasta
1 (15 ounce) can kidney beans
1 (15 ounce) can diced tomatoes
¼ teaspoon pepper

Cook onion in oil 5 minutes. Add seasonings, bouillon cubes, and water. Cover and bring to boil. Add pasta and beans. Reduce heat and simmer 10 minutes. Stir in tomatoes. Cook 5 minutes longer. Serve hot.

BLACK BEAN SOUP

1 (15 ounce) can black beans, drained
1 (10 ounce) can beef broth
1 soup can water
1 cup tomato juice
¼ teaspoon rosemary
¼ teaspoon sweet basil
1 teaspoon lemon juice

Combine all ingredients except lemon juice
and simmer 20 minutes. Add lemon juice after
removing from heat.

CHILI

2 pounds lean ground beef, browned
5 tablespoons chili powder (more or less to taste)
2 cups water
1 onion, finely chopped
2 (15 ounce) cans diced tomatoes
1 (15 ounce) can red beans
1 (15 ounce) can pinto beans

....

Combine all ingredients and simmer 20 to 30 minutes.

POTATO SOUP

5 large potatoes
1 cup sour cream
2 (10 ounce) cans cheddar cheese soup
2½ cups milk
Salt and pepper to taste

Peel and cut potatoes into cubes. Boil potatoes 15 to 20 minutes or until soft. Drain. Add soup and sour cream. Gently mix until blended. Add milk, salt, and pepper. Stir well. Heat on medium heat until soup is warm.

CREATING A KID-FRIENDLY KITCHEN

Consider using plastic measuring cups and mixing bowls when your child helps in the kitchen. These are lighter than glass tools and are less likely to break.

Quick Tip

MACARONI AND CHEESE

1 (12 ounce) container low-fat ricotta cheese
1 (5 ounce) can evaporated milk
½ cup cheddar cheese, shredded
1 teaspoon salt
¼ teaspoon pepper
2 cups macaroni, cooked

....

Add all ingredients to medium saucepan, except macaroni. Heat and stir until cheese melts, about 5 minutes. Fold in macaroni and heat through.

In the Oven

Surround me with your tender mercies so I may live, for your instructions are my delight.
PSALM 119:77 NLT

FRENCH TOAST CASSEROLE

1 (16 ounce) loaf cinnamon raisin bread, cubed
6 large eggs, beaten
3 cups milk
2 teaspoons vanilla extract
Powdered sugar

Layer bread cubes evenly in greased 9x13-inch baking dish. Beat eggs, milk, and vanilla in a separate bowl. Pour mixture over bread cubes. Cover and refrigerate at least 2 hours or overnight. Bake 50 minutes at 350 degrees or until golden brown. Sprinkle with powdered sugar. Serve warm, topped with syrup.

BREAKFAST LASAGNA

½ cup sour cream
1 (10 ounce) can cream of mushroom soup
1 (32 ounce) bag frozen hash browns
1 sweet onion diced
1 pound cooked bacon, diced
1 cup cheddar cheese, shredded
1 cup mozzarella cheese, shredded

Mix sour cream and mushroom soup until well blended. In lasagna pan, layer hash browns, soup/ sour cream mixture, onion, bacon, and cheese. Cover with foil and bake at 325 degrees for 1 hour. Remove foil and bake 5 additional minutes.

TUNA MELTS

1 (5 ounce) can flaked tuna, drained
1 hard-boiled egg, peeled and chopped
2 green onions, chopped
1 tablespoon sweet relish
1 cup cheddar cheese, shredded
¼ cup mayonnaise
1 teaspoon Dijon mustard
4 sandwich buns, split

. . . .

Mix together all ingredients except buns. Spoon mixture into split buns. Wrap each bun tightly in foil. Place in oven and bake 15 minutes at 400 degrees.

CHEESY BROCCOLI AND RICE CASSEROLE

2 cups white rice, cooked
1 (16 ounce) package frozen broccoli, thawed
1 small onion, chopped
2 cups cheddar cheese
1 (10 ounce) can cream of mushroom soup
1 teaspoon Worcestershire sauce
1 teaspoon salt
¼ teaspoon pepper

Mix all ingredients in 9x13-inch casserole dish. Bake at 350 degrees for 25 minutes or until heated through.

TATER TOT CASSEROLE

1 pound ground beef, browned
½ cup frozen peas
½ cup frozen corn
1 (10 ounce) can cream of potato soup
1 (10 ounce) can cream of onion soup
2 cups sharp cheddar cheese, shredded
4 cups frozen tater tots

....

In 9x13-inch casserole dish, mix beef, peas, corn, soups, and 1 cup cheese. Top with tater tots and bake at 350 degrees for 45 minutes or until tots begin to brown. Sprinkle remaining cheese over top and cook for 5 more minutes or until cheese melts.

BROILED PEANUT BUTTER SANDWICHES

1 English muffin per sandwich
1 teaspoon butter per sandwich
1 tablespoon peanut butter per sandwich
1 teaspoon honey per sandwich
Raisins

....

Spread English muffin with butter, peanut butter, and honey. Top with a few raisins. Wrap in foil and broil on low until warm.

IN THE OVEN

CHEESEBURGER AND FRIES CASSEROLE

1 pound frozen french fries, baked according to
  package directions
1 pound ground beef, browned
1 (14 ounce) can sloppy joe mix
2 cups cheddar cheese, shredded

. . . .

Place prepared fries in the bottom of 9x13-inch
casserole dish. Spoon browned hamburger on top
of fries. Add sloppy joe mix. Top with cheese. Bake
in oven at 350 degrees for 30 minutes or until
heated through.

DINNER DEBRIEFING

Allow kids to share what they learned
from their time cooking with you as you
eat together around the dinner table. They
may just discover new talents you didn't
even know they had.

CHICKEN AND NOODLES

IN THE OVEN

2 cups cooked chicken, diced
1 (16 ounce) package thick home-style egg
    noodles, cooked according to package
1 (8 ounce) block processed cheese,
    cut into cubes
2 (10 ounce) cans cream of mushroom soup
1 cup bread crumbs

....

Combine first four ingredients in 9x13-inch
casserole dish. Top with bread crumbs. Cover with
foil. Bake 35 to 40 minutes at 350 degrees.

BISCUIT PIZZA

2 (8 ounce) tubes refrigerated biscuits
2 cups spaghetti sauce
2 cups mozzarella cheese, shredded
Pepperoni

....

Place biscuits in greased baking pan. Press together. Top with sauce, cheese, and desired amount of pepperoni. Bake according to package directions.

BOB'S BAKED BEANS

4 slices bacon, cooked and crumbled
1 small sweet onion, chopped
1 (26 ounce) can vegetarian baked beans
⅓ cup ketchup
2 tablespoons brown sugar
½ teaspoon Worcestershire sauce

....

Combine all ingredients and pour into casserole dish. Bake at 350 degrees for 30 minutes.

LARRY'S ZUCCHINI BAKE

1 onion, chopped
1 tablespoon olive oil
2 medium zucchinis, peeled and sliced
1 (16 ounce) can diced tomatoes
Salt and pepper to taste
2 cups mozzarella cheese, shredded
½ cup bread crumbs

....

Sauté onion in oil. Add zucchini and cook until tender. Add tomatoes, salt, and pepper. Cook 2 minutes. In greased glass baking pan, layer the ingredients like lasagna. Top with bread crumbs. Bake at 350 degrees for 20 minutes.

CREAMY CHICKEN ENCHILADAS

IN THE OVEN

2 cans cream of chicken soup
4 ounces sour cream
1 (7 ounce) can cooked chicken
1 (4 ounce) can diced green chilies
8 corn tortillas
1 cup cheddar cheese, shredded

....

Mix cream of chicken soup, sour cream, chicken, and chilies together in a medium saucepan; cook over medium heat for about 15 minutes, stirring constantly. Fill each tortilla with mixture and roll up. Place them in a row in 9x13-inch casserole dish. Pour any remaining mixture over the tortillas. Sprinkle with cheese. Bake at 350 degrees for 20 minutes or until heated through.

FAMILY ROAST

1 (5 pound) rump roast
3 (10 ounce) cans golden mushroom soup
½ cup water
4 small onions, chopped in large chunks
16 carrots, peeled and sliced
10 medium potatoes
Salt and pepper to taste

In baking pan, place roast, soup, water, and vegetables; add salt and pepper to taste. Cover and bake at 350 degrees. Check roast after 2 hours. Continue baking until tender.

FAST FISH DINNER

14 ounces frozen batter-dipped fish
1 (16 ounce) package frozen french fries
1 (10 ounce) can cream of celery soup
¾ cup milk
⅓ cup mayonnaise
2 tablespoons relish

Place fish on bottom of greased baking dish. Add french fries. Mix all remaining ingredients together. Pour over top of casserole, covering all french fries and fish. Bake at 350 degrees for 45 minutes or until bubbly.

BAKED CHICKEN DINNER

1 (10 ounce) can cream of celery soup
2 cups prepared brown rice
1 (16 ounce) package frozen mixed vegetables
4 to 6 boneless, skinless chicken breasts
1 cup cheddar cheese, shredded

....

Combine soup, rice, and vegetables in a casserole dish. Top with chicken and sprinkle with cheese. Cover with foil and bake at 350 degrees for one hour.

MORE RESPONSIBILITY

As kids grow and mature, you'll be able to give them more diverse tasks in the kitchen. Start by teaching safe and easy tasks like how to mix with a wooden spoon, add ingredients, and clean up the workspace. Always supervise, especially when a new skill is being learned, and offer positive reinforcement when the skill is mastered.

Quick
Tip

SCALLOPED POTATOES

1 (2 pound) package frozen hash browns, thawed
½ cup butter, melted
1 small onion, chopped
1 tablespoon salt
¼ teaspoon pepper
1 (10 ounce) can cream of chicken soup
2 cups sour cream
1 cup cooked ham, diced
2 cups cheddar cheese, shredded
¼ cup butter cracker crumbs

....

In casserole dish, mix all ingredients together except cracker crumbs. Bake at 350 degrees for 40 minutes. Stir. Top with cracker crumbs and bake an additional 5 minutes.

DEEP DISH MEAT PIE

1 pound ground beef
¼ cup onion, chopped
1 (10 ounce) package frozen peas and carrots,
   cooked and drained
1 cup cooked potatoes, chopped
8 ounces processed American cheese, cubed
1 (10 ounce) can cream of mushroom soup
1 (8 ounce) can refrigerated crescent dinner rolls

······································

Brown beef with onion. In greased 9x9-inch baking
pan, mix all ingredients together except rolls.
Separate cresent dough into 4 rectangles; firmly
press together to seal. Place over meat mixture.
Bake at 375 degrees for 20 to 25 minutes or until
golden brown.

CHICKEN AND STUFFING CASSEROLE

1 (8 ounce) package stuffing mix
¼ cup butter, melted
1 (10 ounce) can cream of chicken soup
1 (10 ounce) can cream of celery soup
1 cup chicken broth
2 cups cooked chicken, diced
1½ cups frozen peas
½ onion, minced
Salt and pepper to taste

Mix the stuffing and butter together. Line the bottom of greased 9x13-inch casserole dish with half the stuffing mixture. Combine remaining ingredients in a separate bowl and spread over stuffing. Then spread remaining stuffing on top and gently pat. Bake at 350 degrees for 30 minutes.

TUNA NOODLE CASSEROLE

1 (10 ounce) can cream of celery soup
½ cup milk
1 cup cooked peas
2 (5 ounce) cans tuna, drained
2 cups hot cooked egg noodles
2 tablespoons butter cracker crumbs

Mix all ingredients except crumbs in baking dish. Bake 30 minutes at 350 degrees. Stir. Top with cracker crumbs and bake an additional 5 minutes.

CHICKEN & RICE BAKE

1 (10 ounce) can cream of mushroom soup
1 cup water
¾ cup uncooked minute white rice
⅛ teaspoon pepper
¼ teaspoon garlic salt
4 boneless, skinless chicken breasts

∙∙∙

Mix soup, water, rice, and pepper in shallow baking
dish. Place chicken on rice mixture. Sprinkle with
garlic salt. Cover. Bake at 375 degrees for 45 minutes
or until chicken is no longer pink and rice is done.

IN THE OVEN

BEEF AND NOODLES CASSEROLE

½ pound lean ground beef, browned
1 onion, chopped
1 (15 ounce) can chili without beans
1 (10 ounce) can diced tomatoes, drained
1 (4 ounce) can diced green chilies
2 teaspoons mustard
1 cup elbow macaroni, cooked
1 egg, beaten
1 cup mozzarella cheese, shredded and divided

Combine all ingredients and bake at 350 degrees uncovered, 35 to 40 minutes or until bubbly.

BEEF AND CORN BREAD BAKE

1 pound ground beef
1 teaspoon of oregano
¾ cup salsa
1 (8 ounce) can tomato sauce
1 (16 ounce) can whole kernel corn, drained
½ cup cheddar cheese, shredded
1 (8 ounce) package corn muffin mix,
    prepared according to package, but not baked

....

In large skillet, brown beef with oregano; add salsa, tomato sauce, and corn. Heat through. Stir in cheese. Pour into 9x9-inch baking dish. Spread unbaked corn muffin mixture over meat mixture. Bake 25 to 30 minutes at 375 degrees or until topping is golden brown. Let stand 10 minutes before serving.

PIZZA POCKETS

1 pound ground sausage, browned
1 cup spaghetti sauce
1 teaspoon oregano
½ teaspoon pepper
1 pinch salt
1 cup mozzerella cheese, shredded
1 (8 ounce) tube refrigerated pizza dough

Mix all ingredients together except dough. Roll out and divide dough into four squares. Spoon ¼ of mixture into each square and fold over, sealing edges firmly with fork. Place on ungreased baking sheet. Bake in 350 degree oven for 15 to 20 minutes or until golden brown.

KIDS' APRONS

Don't have kid-sized aprons for your little ones? Tie old (but clean) adult-sized T-shirts around their waists or have them wear old (but clean) adult-sized button-up shirts like a smock.

Quick Tip

OVEN-BAKED SPAGHETTI

1 (16 ounce) package spaghetti, cooked
1 (24 ounce) jar spaghetti sauce
2 cups mozzarella cheese, shredded
8 ounces ricotta cheese
1 teaspoon garlic salt

Mix all ingredients together and bake in covered casserole dish at 350 degrees for 20 minutes.

Snacks, Sweets & Drinks

*Pleasant words are a honeycomb, sweet
to the soul and healing to the bones.*
PROVERBS 16:24 NIV

4 tablespoons flour
4 tablespoons sugar
2 tablespoons cocoa
1 egg
3 tablespoons milk
3 tablespoons oil
3 tablespoons mini chocolate chips
⅛ teaspoon vanilla
Whipped cream

Add dry ingredients to large microwavable mug and mix well. Add the egg and mix thoroughly. Add milk and oil. Mix well. Add chocolate chips and vanilla, and mix again. Microwave 3 minutes on high. The cake will rise over the top of the mug. Allow to cool a little, top with whipped cream, and serve.

Sliced bananas
Graham cracker squares
Large marshmallows
Milk chocolate candy bars

For each snack, top a graham cracker square with a piece of chocolate, 4 banana slices, and a marshmallow. Microwave 10 to 12 seconds or until marshmallow is puffed. Place another graham cracker on top and enjoy.

BROWNIE PIZZA

1 (15 ounce) box fudge brownie mix,
   prepared according to package directions
½ cup peanut butter
½ cup mini chocolate chips
1 (6 ounce) package candy-coated
   milk chocolate pieces

. . . .

Grease 12-inch pizza pan. Pour brownie mix onto
the pizza pan. Bake at 350 for 15 minutes or until
done in center. Remove from oven and let sit 2
minutes. Drop peanut butter and mini chips onto
brownie and let sit 30 seconds or until peanut
butter is melted and easily spreadable. Spread
over brownie and top with candy pieces.

CHOCOLATE TRUFFLES

⅔ cup heavy whipping cream
2 cups semisweet or milk chocolate chips
2 teaspoons vanilla

In saucepan, heat cream almost to a boil. Remove from heat and add chocolate chips. Whisk gently until the chocolate is melted and the mixture is smooth. Stir in vanilla and pour into bowl. Cover and refrigerate 3 hours or until firm. When chocolate mixture is solid enough to work with, scoop into 1-inch balls and roll in your favorite coatings such as crushed cookies, sprinkles, powdered sugar, coconut, chopped nuts, or colored sugars. Cover and refrigerate for 2 hours. Serve cold. Keep refrigerated in an airtight container.

PUPPY CHOW

1 cup chocolate chips
½ cup peanut butter
¼ cup butter
¼ teaspoon vanilla
9 cups toasted oat cereal
1½ cups powdered sugar

. . . .

Combine chocolate chips, peanut butter, and butter in a bowl. Microwave on high 1 minute; stir. If not yet smooth, microwave 30 seconds more. Stir in vanilla. In large bowl, pour mixture over cereal, stirring until all pieces are evenly coated. Place cereal mixture and powdered sugar in large resealable plastic bag. Shake until all pieces are well coated. Spread on waxed paper to cool. Store in resealable plastic bag.

½ cup peanut butter
½ cup honey or corn syrup
¼ cup orange juice
1½ cup nonfat dry milk
4 cups crispy cereal mix

Mix all ingredients thoroughly. Add 4 cups crispy cereal mix. Shape into small balls.

EXTRA SPECIAL CHOCOLATE MILK

1 cup milk
2 tablespoons chocolate syrup
Whipped cream
Candy-coated chocolate pieces or sprinkles

Pour milk into mug. Add syrup and top with desired amount of whipped cream. Top with candy or sprinkles.

Allow your kids to get creative and concoct a new recipe. Try adapting a cookie recipe to include a favorite kind of candy, or a casserole dish with a different kind of cheese or vegetable. You can get as adventurous as you want, but be prepared for a few failures before you get the perfect result.

Quick Tip

KRISTY'S NO-BAKE DELIGHTS

2 cups sugar
3 tablespoons unsweetened cocoa
½ cup margarine
½ cup milk
⅛ teaspoon salt
3 cups quick oats
½ cup peanut butter
1 teaspoon vanilla

In heavy saucepan, bring sugar, cocoa, margarine, milk, and salt to a rapid boil for 1 minute. Add quick oats, peanut butter, and vanilla; mix well. Working quickly, drop by spoonful onto waxed paper and let cool.

1 cup creamy peanut butter
1 stick butter
1¾ cups powdered sugar
1 (12 ounce) package milk chocolate chips

Mix peanut butter and butter until creamy. Add sugar gradually. Refrigerate for 30 minutes. Roll peanut butter mixture into 1-inch balls. Set on cookie sheets covered with waxed paper and freeze until firm. Melt chocolate in microwave on high for 2 minutes. Do not overheat. Stir. Insert toothpick into frozen peanut butter ball and dip into chocolate to almost cover the entire ball. Let cool on waxed paper. Keep refrigerated.

MANDARIN ORANGE PIE

1 cup whipped cream
2 cups orange flavored yogurt
½ cup canned mandarin orange slices, drained
1 graham cracker pie shell

. . . .

Fold whipped cream into yogurt in large bowl. Stir in oranges. Pour into pie shell. Cover with plastic wrap. Let chill at least 3 hours in refrigerator before serving. You can also freeze this pie and thaw slightly before serving.

CHOCOLATE DRIZZLED KETTLE CORN

2 bags microwave kettle corn
½ cup semisweet or milk chocolate chips

Pop bags of microwave kettle corn and spread in large baking pan. Microwave chocolate chips on high for 30 seconds. Stir. Repeat until chips are melted. Dip a fork into chocolate and drizzle over kettle corn. Allow to cool before serving.

3 cups semisweet chocolate chips
1 (14 ounce) can sweetened condensed milk
1 teaspoon vanilla

In large microwavable bowl, combine chocolate chips and sweetened condensed milk. Microwave on high for 2 minutes. Add vanilla. Stir. Line 8x8-inch pan with waxed paper and pour in fudge. Refrigerate.

PEANUT BUTTER PIE

¾ cup powdered sugar
⅓ cup peanut butter
1 refrigerated pie shell, baked
1 (8 ounce) box vanilla pudding, prepared
2 cups whipped topping

In small bowl, use pastry blender to combine powdered sugar and peanut butter; set aside. Line pie shell with ⅓ of peanut butter mixture. Spread pudding evenly on top. Top with whipped topping and sprinkle remaining peanut butter mixture evenly over the pie. Chill well.

2 tablespoons cinnamon
½ cup sugar
4 pieces bread
Butter

. . . .

Mix together cinnamon and sugar. Toast bread
and spread with butter. Sprinkle cinnamon/sugar
mixture evenly over top.

8 ounces whipped topping
16 ounces strawberry yogurt
1 graham cracker pie shell

Fold whipped topping into yogurt in large bowl.
Pour into pie shell. Let chill at least 3 hours in
refrigerator before serving.

Have your kids plan a special themed dinner for your family. The evening could center on a cuisine type (Mexican, Italian, All-American), a color (green eggs and ham, anyone?), or a letter of the alphabet (a *B* meal could be made up of burgers, beans, baked apples, and brownies for dessert). If you're feeling extra festive, have your kids decorate the table in keeping with the dinner theme.

Quick Tip

CRUNCHY CHOCOLATE COOKIES

1 cup chow mein noodles
2 cups mini marshmallows
2 cups oats
1 (12 ounce) bag chocolate chips
1 (12 ounce) bag peanut butter chips

. . . .

Combine noodles, marshmallows, and oats in large bowl. Stir. In separate bowl, microwave chocolate and peanut butter chips in 30-second intervals until melted. Pour over noodle mixture and stir to coat. Spoon clumps onto wax paper and cool.

1 ¼ cups vanilla wafers, crushed
½ cup flaked coconut
¾ cup powdered sugar
3 ounces frozen orange juice concentrate, thawed
Additional powdered sugar

Mix together the vanilla wafers, coconut, ¾ cup powdered sugar, and orange juice concentrate. Shape into 1-inch balls and roll in powdered sugar. Store covered in the refrigerator.

Clear plastic cups
Prepared chocolate pudding
6 chocolate sandwich cookies, crushed
Gummy worms

. . . .

Layer pudding and crushed cookies in clear plastic cups. Hide worms throughout layers and place 1 to 2 on top.

PEANUT BUTTER LOGS

1¾ cups powdered sugar
¼ cup butter
1 cup crunchy peanut butter
2 cups crisp rice cereal

Combine powdered sugar and butter in large bowl and beat until smooth. Stir in peanut butter and cereal. Shape dough into finger-sized logs. Place logs onto cookie sheet lined with waxed paper. Refrigerate 1 hour. If desired, spread with prepared chocolate frosting. Keep refrigerated.

ROOT BEER FLOAT

1 cup root beer
1 scoop vanilla ice cream

. . . .

Place root beer in large glass and add ice cream.
Try this with other flavors of soda and ice cream
such as cola and chocolate ice cream or orange
soda and pineapple sherbet.

FROZEN FRUIT POPSICLES

Plastic cups
Various fruit juices
Canned peaches, pears, or mandarin oranges

Fill the plastic cup halfway with your favorite fruit juice. Add chunks of fruit and freeze. Halfway through freezing, place a Popsicle stick in the center. Freeze until solid.

FROZEN APPLESAUCE FRUIT SNACK

1 cup apple sauce
1 (10 ounce) package frozen strawberries, thawed
1 (11 ounce) can mandarin oranges, drained
2 tablespoons orange juice

. . . .

Combine all ingredients in large bowl. Spoon
fruit mixture into paper cups. Freeze until firm.
Remove from freezer about 30 minutes before
serving.

1 (8 ounce) package refrigerated crescent rolls
Prepared vanilla pudding cups

Find a stick that is about 2 inches in diameter and wrap it in foil. Wrap crescent roll around stick to form a cone. Cook over the fire until light brow. Allow to cool. Remove from stick and spoon vanilla pudding into center. This is fun to do while camping or in the backyard!

Preparing food for people who need it is a great way to involve your kids in sharing with others. Consider preparing snacks to take to a nursing home or volunteering to provide a meal for a local homeless shelter or halfway house. As a family, help to distribute this food to others and remember these people in your family prayer time.

Quick
Tip

SNACKS, SWEETS & DRINKS

1 (14 ounce) can sweetened condensed milk
1 (6 ounce) can frozen lemonade concentrate,
    thawed
1 (8 ounce) container whipped cream, thawed
1 graham cracker piecrust

Beat together condensed milk and lemonade.
Gently fold in whipped cream. Pour into piecrust.
Freeze 4 hours or until firm.